e Study

JOHN'S LETTERS
Discovering Genuine Christianity

**12 studies
for individuals or groups**

Ron Blankley

With Notes for Leaders

IVP Connect

An imprint of InterVarsity Press
Downers Grove, Illinois

InterVarsity Press
P.O. Box 1400, Downers Grove, IL 60515-1426
World Wide Web: www.ivpress.com
E-mail: mail@ivpress.com
©*1990, 2002 by Ronald A. Blankley*

InterVarsity Press® *is the book-publishing division of InterVarsity Christian Fellowship/USA*®*, a student movement active on campus at hundreds of universities, colleges and schools of nursing in the United States of America, and a member movement of the International Fellowship of Evangelical Students. For information about local and regional activities, write Public Relations Dept., InterVarsity Christian Fellowship/USA, 6400 Schroeder Rd., P.O. Box 7895, Madison, WI 53707-7895, or visit the IVCF website at <www.intervarsity.org>.*

LifeGuide® *is a registered trademark of InterVarsity Christian Fellowship.*

All Scripture quotations, unless otherwise indicated, are taken from the Holy Bible, New International Version®. NIV®. *Copyright* ©*1973, 1978, 1984 by International Bible Society. Used by permission of Zondervan Publishing House. All rights reserved.*

Cover photograph: Dennis Flaherty

ISBN-10: 0-8308-3020-0
ISBN-13: 978-0-8308-3020-6

Printed in the United States of America ∞

P	22	21	20	19	18	17	16	15	14	13	12	11	10	9	8	7	6
Y	20	19	18	17	16	15	14	13	12	11	10	09	08	07	06		

Contents

Getting the Most Out of
John's Letters

In one of his Breakpoint commentaries Charles Colson focuses on the confusion that exists among today's Baby Boomers over what it means to be "born again." He says:

> Wade Clark Roof is the author of a new book called *Spiritual Marketplace: Baby Boomers and the Remaking of American Religion.* A religious studies professor, Roof says that one-third of America's 77 million Baby Boomers identify themselves as "born again Christians." The question is, what do they mean by this?[1]

That's a great question, especially in light of the fact that the book goes on to state that only about half of those who call themselves "born again" today attend a conservative Protestant church. Twenty percent don't belong to any church. Shockingly, a third of these who say they're "born again" believe in astrology and reincarnation.

How are we to respond to this news? In a culture in which so many are calling themselves born-again Christians, how can we tell the difference between genuine Christians and those who merely profess to know Christ?

John's letters were written for that very purpose. John writes to expose the false claims of those whose conduct contradicts their claims. He also provides strong assurance to those whose lifestyle is consistent with their Christian faith.

Background to 1 John

First John was written between A.D. 85 and 95 by the apostle John, the author of the Gospel of John and Revelation. Evidently the letter was

---

[1]Charles Colson, CNS Commentary from "Breakpoint," February 16, 2000.

circulated among a number of churches in Asia that were threatened by false teachers. These false teachers embraced an early form of heresy known as Gnosticism. They taught that matter was entirely evil and spirit was entirely good. This teaching resulted in two fundamental errors.

A "new" theology. This centered in a denial of the incarnation. Since God could not be contaminated by a human body, these false teachers did not believe God became a man in Jesus Christ. Some taught that he merely seemed to have a body, a view known as Docetism. Others claimed that the divine Christ descended on Jesus at his baptism but departed before the crucifixion, a view known as Cerinthianism. This latter view seems to be in the background of much of 1 John.

A "new" morality. These false teachers also claimed "to have reached such an advanced stage in spiritual experience that they were 'beyond good and evil.' They maintained that they had no sin, not in the sense that they had attained moral perfection but in the sense that what might be sin for people at a less mature stage of inner development was no longer sin for the completely 'spiritual' man. For him ethical distinctions had ceased to be relevant."[2]

What intensified this problem was that these false teachers had once been an active part of the fellowship which John's readers were continuing to enjoy (see 1 John 2:19). But because their "new" teaching was so contrary to the apostolic truths of the gospel, they had to part company with the faithful. As you can well imagine, those who remained in the true fellowship were unsettled and shaken by the defection of these new teachers and needed to be reassured. But in the process, the others also needed to be exposed for what they truly were—unbelieving heretics.

In order to accomplish both purposes, John provides a series of tests for distinguishing between genuine Christians and those who falsely claim to know Christ. In response to the "new" theology, he provides us with a doctrinal test: What does the person believe about Christ? In response to the "new" morality, he provides us with a moral test: How does the person respond to the commandments of

---

[2] F. F. Bruce, *The Epistles of John* (Grand Rapids, Mich.: Eerdmans, 1979), p. 26.

Christ? Finally, he provides us with a social test: Does the person love other Christians?

In fact, John's entire first letter is structured around these three tests, each of which appears in three separate groups, or cycles, in the letter. After the prologue (1:1-4), there is the first cycle (1:5—2:27), followed by the second (2:28—4:6) and third (4:7—5:12). Then in the conclusion (5:13-21), John again emphasizes his theme of Christian assurance.

In view of this purpose and structure, it is important to realize that the contrasts in John's letter are not between two types of Christians but between genuine Christians and those who merely claim to be Christians. For in the words of John Stott, "John's argument is double-edged. If he seeks to bring believers to the knowledge that they have eternal life, he is equally at pains to show that unbelievers have not. His purpose is to destroy the false assurance of the counterfeit as well as to confirm the right assurance of the genuine."[3]

Background to 2 John

Second John was also written by the apostle John between A.D. 85 and 95 to provide guidance about hospitality. During the first century, traveling evangelists relied on the hospitality of church members. Because inns were few and unsafe, believers would take such people into their homes and then give them provisions for their journey. Since Gnostic teachers also relied on hospitality, John warned his readers against taking such people into their homes lest they participate in spreading heresy.

Background to 3 John

Third John was also written to provide us with guidance about hospitality, but in a much more positive way. Whereas 2 John tells us what we are *not* to do, 3 John emphasizes what we *are* to do. For those genuine teachers who are totally dependent on the body of Christ for all of their needs, we are to open not only our hearts but also our homes. This instruction is primarily found in John's commendation of Gaius,

---

[3]John Stott, *The Epistles of John* (Grand Rapids, Mich.: Eerdmans, 1974), p. 52.

who has done this very thing, and in his denunciation of Diotrephes, who has refused. These two men become living examples of good and evil, truth and error.

This LifeGuide Bible Study contains twelve studies in John's letters. The first ten cover 1 John, and the next two look at 2 and 3 John. There is also an optional review study of the three books. It is my hope that these studies will encourage and assure you that you "walk in the truth."

Suggestions for Individual Study

1. As you begin each study, pray that God will speak to you through his Word.

2. Read the introduction to the study and respond to the personal reflection question or exercise. This is designed to help you focus on God and on the theme of the study.

3. Each study deals with a particular passage—so that you can delve into the author's meaning in that context. Read and reread the passage to be studied. The questions are written using the language of the New International Version, so you may wish to use that version of the Bible. The New Revised Standard Version is also recommended.

4. This is an inductive Bible study, designed to help you discover for yourself what Scripture is saying. The study includes three types of questions. *Observation* questions ask about the basic facts: who, what, when, where and how. *Interpretation* questions delve into the meaning of the passage. *Application* questions help you discover the implications of the text for growing in Christ. These three keys unlock the treasures of Scripture.

Write your answers to the questions in the spaces provided or in a personal journal. Writing can bring clarity and deeper understanding of yourself and of God's Word.

5. It might be good to have a Bible dictionary handy. Use it to look up any unfamiliar words, names or places.

6. Use the prayer suggestion to guide you in thanking God for what you have learned and to pray about the applications that have come to mind.

7. You may want to go on to the suggestion under "Now or Later," or you may want to use that idea for your next study.

Suggestions for Members of a Group Study

1. Come to the study prepared. Follow the suggestions for individual study mentioned above. You will find that careful preparation will greatly enrich your time spent in group discussion.

2. Be willing to participate in the discussion. The leader of your group will not be lecturing. Instead, he or she will be encouraging the members of the group to discuss what they have learned. The leader will be asking the questions that are found in this guide.

3. Stick to the topic being discussed. Your answers should be based on the verses which are the focus of the discussion and not on outside authorities such as commentaries or speakers. These studies focus on a particular passage of Scripture. Only rarely should you refer to other portions of the Bible. This allows for everyone to participate in in-depth study on equal ground.

4. Be sensitive to the other members of the group. Listen attentively when they describe what they have learned. You may be surprised by their insights! Each question assumes a variety of answers. Many questions do not have "right" answers, particularly questions that aim at meaning or application. Instead the questions push us to explore the passage more thoroughly.

When possible, link what you say to the comments of others. Also, be affirming whenever you can. This will encourage some of the more hesitant members of the group to participate.

5. Be careful not to dominate the discussion. We are sometimes so eager to express our thoughts that we leave too little opportunity for others to respond. By all means participate! But allow others to also.

6. Expect God to teach you through the passage being discussed and through the other members of the group. Pray that you will have an enjoyable and profitable time together, but also that as a result of the study you will find ways that you can take action individually and/or as a group.

7. Remember that anything said in the group is considered confidential and should not be discussed outside the group unless specific permission is given to do so.

8. If you are the group leader, you will find additional suggestions at the back of the guide.

1

Fellowship & Forgiveness

1 John 1

Most professing Christians seem to be interested in fellowship. They gather in fellowship halls, attend fellowship dinners and participate in well-organized activities and groups. But what is it that makes genuine Christian fellowship possible? More important, how can we know that we have genuine fellowship with God?

GROUP DISCUSSION. What normally comes to your mind when you think of fellowship with others?

fellowship with God?

PERSONAL REFLECTION. What are some of the barriers you have experienced to deepening your fellowship with others and with God?

John begins this first letter with a prologue (vv. 1-4), in which he presents to his readers the basis for fellowship with God the Father, God the Son, the apostles and Christians in general. He then goes on to present the first of a series of tests by which we can determine if we have fellowship with God (vv. 5-10). *Read 1 John 1.*

1. John begins this chapter by announcing an apostolic message. What is the content of this message (vv. 1-2)?

2. What would it have been like to be the bearer of this message?

3. What are John's reasons for announcing his message (vv. 3-4)?

4. In light of this apostolic message, what is the foundation of our fellowship as Christians?

Why is this so essential?

5. Describe the test John is using to determine if we have fellowship with God (vv. 5-10).

6. The basis for this test is God's character (v. 5). What specifically do *light* and *darkness* symbolize (vv. 5-7; see John 3:19-21)?

7. The first part of John's test concerns the way we live or "walk" (vv. 6-7). What type of person is John describing here?

8. The second part of John's test concerns our attitude toward sin (vv. 8-10). What does our denial or confession of sin reveal about the reality of our relationship with God?

9. What attitudes in your own heart and life does this text bring to light?

10. Based on your study of this passage, what does it mean to have fellowship with God and each other?

11. Does John's test strengthen or weaken your assurance of fellowship with God? Explain.

Pray that God might use this passage to encourage you to demonstrate the reality of your fellowship with God.

Now or Later

What steps could you take to enjoy a greater fellowship with those who also know the Father and the Son?

2

Talking &
Walking the Truth

From the very beginning of Jesus' ministry, he emphasized that it is not merely what we profess that counts for eternity. In his first major message he declared, "Not everyone who says to me, 'Lord, Lord,' will enter the kingdom of heaven, but only he who does the will of my Father who is in heaven" (Matthew 7:21).

GROUP DISCUSSION. When people we know say one thing yet do another, which do you think usually reveals the truth about them? Why?

PERSONAL REFLECTION. In what ways can you bring your actions more in line with your beliefs?

John emphasizes that our claim to know Christ must be backed by our conduct. Both are necessary if we are to be certain about the reality of our faith. Within these verses, John first continues the theme he began in the previous passage (1:5-10): genuine fellowship with God causes us to oppose sin (2:1-2) and obey the commands of Christ

(2:3-6). He then goes on to relate such obedience to one command in particular: love the brethren (2:7-11). *Read 1 John 2:1-11.*

---

1. Although John does not want us to sin, he reminds us of God's provision when we do (vv. 1-2). What is the relationship between Christ speaking to the Father "in our defense" (v. 1) and his "atoning sacrifice" on our behalf (v. 2)?

---

2. How does this understanding provide comfort and assurance when you do sin?

---

3. According to John, how can we tell whether we truly know Christ or merely claim to know him (vv. 3-6)?

---

4. What other conclusions does John make about those who obey Christ's commands (vv. 5-6)?

---

5. Practically speaking, what does it mean to "walk as Jesus did" (v. 6)?

---

6. In verses 7-11, John focuses on one of the commands. How can this command be both old and new (vv. 7-8)?

7. Why would love for our brother rather than love for God serve as a test of being in the light (vv. 9-11)?

8. Compare John's statements about love and hate (vv. 9-11) with similar ones made later in the epistle (3:10, 14-15). How do these verses clarify the two types of people John is contrasting?

9. In view of the overall context of this passage, what does it mean to live in the light (v. 10)?

10. What particular areas of your life would you like to bring into the light?

What barriers do you face in doing so?

Pray for a greater consistency in your Christian life.

Now or Later
How does this passage encourage you to obey Christ and love other members of his body?

3

Encouragement & Warning

1 John 2:12-17

Pilgrim's Progress is the classic tale of a Christian's escape from the City of Destruction to the Heavenly City. It is true to experience because all of us can identify with his encounters along the way. In the Valley of Humiliation he enters into combat with Apollyon, his fiercest foe. At the Hill of Difficulty he meets Adam-the-First and his three daughters: Lust-of-the-Flesh, Lust-of-the-Eyes and Pride-of-Life. In the town of Folly he narrowly escapes its greatest attraction, Vanity Fair. These encounters are John Bunyan's well-known descriptions of the threefold arena of all Christian conflict—the world, the flesh and the devil.

GROUP DISCUSSION. How far did you progress as a Christian before you became aware of these three foes? Explain.

PERSONAL REFLECTION. Which of these three foes has proven to be the most troublesome? Why?

Bunyan's foes are the same three enemies that appear in this section of 1 John. These verses are a distinct digression from the flow of thought in the preceding passage. John now pauses to encourage his readers concerning their spiritual condition and to warn them of the entice-ments of the world. *Read 1 John 2:12-17.*

---

1. Why would John want to give a word of encouragement at this point in his letter (vv. 12-14)?

---

2. Who is represented by the three groups being addressed (vv. 12-14)?

How are you encouraged by what John says to each group?

---

3. What is the source of our victory over the evil one (vv. 13-14)?

On a daily basis, how can that truth help us overcome his tactics and schemes?

---

4. Compare John's warning against worldliness (vv. 15-17) with what he says about the world elsewhere (2:2; 3:13; 4:4-5; 5:4-5, 19). What is the meaning of the word *world* here?

5. What is the first reason we are urged not to love the world (vv. 15-16)?

_____

6. How does this realization lessen the appeal of the world in your life?

_____

7. The three worldly desires of verse 16 point us to the problem of the enemy within. How does this emphasis help us to understand the true nature of worldliness?

_____

8. What is the second reason we are not to love the world (v. 17)?

_____

9. How does this realization lessen the world's appeal in your life?

Praise God for giving you the ongoing strength to overcome each of these three foes.

Now or Later

Take a few minutes to journal about how this passage has helped you gain a better understanding of the spiritual battle you face.

4

How Important
Is Theology?

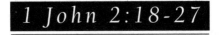

1 John 2:18-27

There is an increasingly popular mindset within the church today which seeks to divorce Christian teaching from Christian living. "We don't want more theology," we are told, "just more about Jesus." But how can we learn more about Jesus apart from a proper understanding of who he is and what he has accomplished? The fact is, there is nothing more basic to Christianity than the person and work of Christ. Apart from understanding the truth about Christ, there can be no real Christian living.

GROUP DISCUSSION. What false views about Jesus Christ are popular today?

PERSONAL REFLECTION. In what ways have you been (or might you be) influenced by false teachers?

In these verses John provides a sharp contrast between true believers and false teachers (vv. 18-21) and gives a fundamental test to distinguish between the two (vv. 22-23). Most important, he establishes that the way to combat error is to continue in the truth (vv. 24-28). *Read 1 John 2:18-27.*

1. What characteristics of false teachers and their teaching is John exposing in these verses?

2. Are there any factors that could make this kind of teaching appealing to you?

3. All the New Testament authors viewed the first coming of Christ as the event that marked the beginning of the end—"the last hour." What are some of the signs of the last hour (vv. 18-19)?

4. What does John tell us about the relationship between our presence in the church and our perseverance in the faith (v. 19)?

5. Truth is the most effective defense against an onslaught of error. What is the "anointing" that gives us such knowledge of the truth (vv. 20-21; also v. 27)?

6. To deny that "Jesus is the Christ" (v. 22) is to deny that the man Jesus is the eternal, divine Christ—the God-man. Why is John so harsh toward those who believe and teach such a view (vv. 22-23)?

7. Why is remaining in the truth so important in the Christian life (vv. 24-25)?

8. Obviously John is not suggesting that all human teachers are unnecessary (v. 27) or else he would not have written this epistle. In light of the problem he is addressing, what then is he saying?

9. How does his instruction (v. 27) help us understand what it means to remain in Christ?

10. What actions or attitudes help (or would help) you to remain in Christ?

Ask God to continue to fill your heart and mind with the truth about his Son.

Now or Later

11. What does this passage teach us about the Holy Spirit's ministry of preserving us from error?

12. What does it teach about our responsibility of persevering in the truth?

5

Like Father,
Like Son

1 John 2:28—3:10

"Born again" was a popular catch-phrase in the 1970s. It is even the title of Charles Colson's popular autobiography. One survey at the time revealed that over fifty million Americans said that they had been "born again," indicating that they had made a decision to trust Christ.[1]

GROUP DISCUSSION. What do you think your local community would be like if one third of everyone who lived there was born again?

PERSONAL REFLECTION. Think of some ways you exhibit your parents' character simply because you share their nature.

In these verses John is demonstrating that those who are born of a righteous God will live a righteous life. Positively, they will continue in obedience (2:28—3:3). Negatively, they will not continue in sin (3:4-10). *Read 1 John 2:28—3:10.*

1. Based on John's emphasis at the beginning and the end of the passage (2:28-29; 3:9-10), what test is he using to validate a person's claim of being born again?

2. As one who has been born of God, what are some ways you can see the family trait of righteousness developing in your life?

3. In unfolding this test, John associates it closely with the "appearing" of Christ (2:28; 3:2-3). Why is our continuance in Christ the basis of our confidence at his coming (2:28)?

4. J. I. Packer writes, "The New Testament gives us two yardsticks of measuring God's love. The first is the cross (see Romans 5:8; 1 John 4:8-10); the second is the gift of sonship."[2] How does the realization that we are God's children help us grasp the greatness of his love for us (3:1)?

Have you been able to get a sense of God's love for you? What has been helpful, and what has made it difficult?

5. How does the hope (confident assurance) of Christ's appearing (3:2-3) serve as a purifying influence in your life?

6. How does John's definition of sin (3:4) compare with some of the viewpoints people have today?

7. Why is it impossible for any follower of Christ to continue in sin (3:5-8)?

8. What specifically is the deception John warns against in this passage (3:7)?

9. Why does the new birth make it impossible for God's children to have a life characterized by sin (3:9)?

10. Since the universal fatherhood of God is not taught in Scripture, our spiritual parentage is either from God or the devil. How do we know which family we belong to (3:10)?

11. What are some things you might need to change in your life to better reflect that you truly are born of God?

Pray that your family resemblance to God and to Christ would be increased.

Now or Later

Recall the situation of your own experience of spiritual birth. Write a prayer of praise and thanksgiving for your earthly and heavenly spiritual parents.

---

[1]"Born Again," *Newsweek*, October 25, 1976, p. 68.
[2]J. I. Packer, *Knowing God* (Downers Grove, Ill.: InterVarsity Press, 1973), p. 194.

6

Blessed
Assurance

1 John 3:11-24

In his classic book *Holiness*, J. C. Ryle expresses concern for believers who doubt: "I heartily wish that assurance was more sought after than it is. Too many among those who believe begin doubting and go on doubting, live doubting and die doubting, and go to heaven in a kind of mist."

He goes onto say, "Doubts and fears have power to spoil much of the happiness of a true believer in Christ. Uncertainty and suspense are bad enough in any condition—in the matter of our health, our property, our families, our affections, our earthly callings—but never so bad as in the affairs of our souls."[1]

Without question, doubt and fear have robbed many of the joy of Christian assurance.

GROUP DISCUSSION. Have you ever questioned whether you were a member of God's family? Explain.

PERSONAL REFLECTION. When do you have the greatest assurance that you are one of God's children?

In these verses John once again points us to love as a test of genuine salvation (vv. 11-14), then provides us with a test of genuine love (vv. 16-18). He concludes this section by demonstrating that the result of our genuine love for one another is assurance and confidence before God (vv. 19-24). *Read 1 John 3:11-24.*

1. What thoughts and feelings do you have as you read these words about love?

2. Why is our love for fellow Christians so basic to our assurance of eternal life (vv. 11-15)?

3. How do verses 14-15 answer those of us who may claim that assurance is based solely on our profession of faith?

4. A popular song says, "Everybody loves somebody sometime." But what is the test of *genuine* love (vv. 16-18)?

5. Why is Christ's death on the cross the supreme example of love (v. 16)?

6. In verses 17-18 John mentions ways we can follow Christ's example. How have you and those in your church sought to love those with material needs?

7. How can John's assurances in verses 19-20 help us deal with times of doubt?

8. Why would our obedience of God's commands affect our confidence in prayer (vv. 21-22)?

9. Why do you think John reduces the commandments to a single command to be obeyed (v. 23)?

10. Both outwardly and inwardly, how can we know Christ lives in us (v. 24)?

How are both types of assurance important to you?

Pray about the needs on your heart with confidence before God.

Now or Later

Based on this passage, how would you counsel someone who lacked assurance that he or she was a Christian?

---

[1]J. C. Ryle, *Holiness* (Grand Rapids, Mich.: Baker, 1979), pp. 158-59.

7

Discernment
& Devotion

1 John 4:1-12

Every Christian virtue bears within itself the seeds of its own destruction. A zeal for the truth, for example, if not tempered by love and compassion, can cause us to become arrogant, harsh and cold. Likewise, love for others, if unchecked by the truth, can cause us to be tolerant toward sin. If one of these virtues is not governed by the other, it can become a liability and not a strength. Like everything else, obtaining a proper balance is of utmost importance.

GROUP DISCUSSION. A sign outside a large urban church says, "Everyone welcome. We are an inclusive community." In a day when pluralism is popular, what messages might this sign be communicating?

PERSONAL REFLECTION. When you see another believer following a teaching you know to be untrue, have you spoken up or have you felt you could not say anything? Reflect on various approaches you might take.

In the first part of this passage, John continues to insist that Christians are those who believe the truth about Christ, in contrast to those who do not (vv. 1-6). Then, without any transition, he reemphasizes that Christians are also those who love others, in contrast to those who do not (vv. 7-12) *Read 1 John 4:1-12.*

---

1. Why is there such a great need for Christians to be discerning (v. 1)?

In what ways is this true for us today?

---

2. What test does John give us for determining whether a person's teaching is from "the Spirit of God" or the "spirit of the antichrist" (vv. 2-3)?

---

3. Have you ever been confronted with a modern-day representative of "the spirit of the antichrist"? Explain.

---

4. As Christians, how can we overcome the doctrinal errors that continually confront us (v. 4)?

---

5. John provides an additional test for discerning whether a person's teaching is "from the world" or "from God" (vv. 5-6). Give some examples of how the makeup of the audience a teacher attracts is indicative of the teacher's own nature or beliefs.

6. Why must we be diligent in our devotion to one another (vv. 7-8)?

7. How does the cross of Christ demonstrate the manner in which "God so loved us" (vv. 9-11)?

8. How does God's love for you motivate you to love those who might be difficult to love (v. 11)?

9. How does our love for each other make the invisible God visible in our midst (v. 12)?

10. In what practical way can you show love this week to a brother or sister in Christ, or demonstrate a greater discernment as you listen to teaching about Christ?

Pray that God might fill you with both love and discernment on a continual basis.

Now or Later

Give further reflection to verse 6. Do you know someone who speaks God's truth in such a way that you feel compelled to listen? What is this person like? Ask God to help you develop these qualities.

8

Fear's Remedy

1 John 4:13-21

In the sequel to *Pilgrim's Progress*, Mr. Great-heart and Father Honest engage in a conversation about an old friend, Mr. Fearing. At one point in the dialogue he is portrayed in the following way: "He was a man that had the root of the matter in him, but he was one of the most troublesome Pilgrims that I ever met with in all my days."

That is Bunyan's way of describing many who are on the road to heaven: thoroughly sincere (the root of the matter is in them) yet so overloaded with doubts and fears that their pilgrimage is indeed "troublesome."

GROUP DISCUSSION. Why do you think fear can so easily overcome us?

PERSONAL REFLECTION. In what ways do you feel burdened by fear?

In these verses John proceeds to explain what he has just taught at the end of the last passage (v. 12): God dwelling in us (vv. 13-16) is demonstrated by our mutual love for one another (vv. 17-21). In the process he also explains why love is the antidote for fear. *Read 1 John 4:13-21.*

---

1. What three assurances does John give for determining that "we live in him and he in us" (vv. 13-16)?

---

2. Which of these three are you most thankful for? Why?

---

3. According to John, how is our testimony about Christ related to our experience of God's presence and love (vv. 14-16)?

---

4. Why does our love for others enable us to be confident on the day of judgment (vv. 17-18)?

---

5. What insights does verse 18 give us into why we sometimes fear God and others?

---

6. How can the principle "perfect love drives out fear" (v. 18) help us overcome our fears?

7. If we have difficulty loving other Christians, what might be the root of the problem (v. 18)?

How have you seen this to be true?

_____

8. Why is it true that we as believers will indeed learn to love other believers (vv. 19-21)?

How have you seen this to be true?

_____

9. In what ways would you like this passage to strengthen your confidence before God?

Pause to voice your fears to God and to listen for his assurances through this passage.

Now or Later

What do you fear? Take some time to list everything you can think of. Then find a way to give these things to God one by one. You might write them on paper and then tear them up. Or you could make a list and cross each one off as you pray about it. Then spend some time in silence, and listen for God's word of comfort and assurance.

9

Faith Is
the Victory

1 John 5:1-12

Christians with a variety of theological views have wholeheartedly sung the words to the well-known hymn: "Faith is the victory! Faith is the victory! O glorious victory, that overcomes the world." But in light of the daily battles in the Christian life, not all agree on what this victory is, when it is accomplished or how we go about achieving it.

GROUP DISCUSSION. What spiritual battles require the focus of your attention?

PERSONAL REFLECTION. In which spiritual battles are you seeing the greatest victory?

In this passage John clears up some of our confusion about faith. First and foremost, overcoming faith is centered in a correct understanding of who Christ is. In the opening five verses of this passage, John demonstrates how belief, obedience and love for God and fellow believers are all related. Then in verses 6-12 he once again sets before us the absolute necessity of believing the truth about God's Son for all who claim to be Christians. *Read 1 John 5:1-12.*

1. What are some inevitable results of the new birth (vv. 1-2)?

2. How have you seen these results in your experience?

3. Why is obedience to God's commandments not burdensome for Christians (v. 3)?

How then can we explain the struggle we sometimes have to obey?

4. Reflect for a moment on the two major characteristics of the world described earlier (see 2:15-17; 4:1-6). What then does it mean for us to "overcome the world" (vv. 4-5)?

5. The heretics of John's day taught that the divine Christ descended on Jesus at his baptism but left before his death (v. 6). What is wrong with this view?

6. How does the fact that Jesus Christ came by water (symbolizing his baptism) and blood (symbolizing his death) refute that heresy (v. 6)?

---

7. The Old Testament law required two or three witnesses to prove a claim. Who are John's three witnesses, and what do they testify (vv. 7-8)?

---

8. Why should we accept this threefold testimony concerning God's Son (v. 9)?

---

9. How does your own experience confirm the truth that eternal life is found only in God's Son (vv. 10-12)?

---

10. How does this passage help you to understand the significance of being born again?

Take time to thank God for his Son and for the victory and eternal life we have in him.

Now or Later

Reread verses 1-5. In what area of your life are you being called to obedience? What steps do you need to take toward that goal?

10

What We Know as Christians

Almost immediately after his well-known conversion experience at Aldersgate Street, John Wesley struggled for months over the uncertainty of his own salvation. Receiving little help from his friends or his church, his thoughts began to turn inward. Focusing on his sinful failures, he became increasingly despondent and dejected. He sought relief by opening passages within the Bible at random, but when that also proved unfruitful he continued his downward spiral. Finally he sank to such depths of despair that he made the following shocking notation in his journal: "My friends affirm that I am mad because I said I was not a Christian a year ago. I affirm I am not a Christian now."[1]

GROUP DISCUSSION. How well can you relate to Wesley's experience? Explain.

PERSONAL REFLECTION. When are those times that you have the least assurance of your salvation?

As John brings this epistle to a close, he again focuses on a number of truths that we can "know" with certainty. *Read 1 John 5:13-21.*

1. Verse 13 is a summary statement of purpose for the entire epistle. What then are those "things" which assure us we have eternal life?

---

2. How have the things referred to in verse 13 helped you gain a greater assurance of your own salvation?

---

3. How can we be assured that our prayers will be answered (vv. 14-15; see also 3:21-22)?

---

4. Verses 16-17 provide one illustration of the kind of prayer that can be made with confidence. Who should we be praying for? Why?

---

5. In light of the whole context of this epistle, what might be the distinction between the sin that does not lead to death and the one that does?

---

6. Why would John not encourage prayer for a person involved in the sin that leads to death?

---

7. Another New Testament author writes, "Your enemy the devil prowls around like a roaring lion looking for someone to devour"

(1 Peter 5:8). In light of this danger, how are you encouraged by John's assurance in verses 18-19?

8. How do we know we belong to God's family and not the world's (v. 19)?

9. How does the coming of God's Son enable us to know the true God in contrast to the false conceptions of God that continually surround us (vv. 20-21)?

10. What certainties in this passage are the most encouraging to you?

Pray that God would make each of these assurances real in your life.

Now or Later

Now that you have completed the studies on 1 John, take time to read through the whole book in one sitting. What themes stand out to you?

What is the most important teaching for you to learn from this book?

---

[1]Arnold A. Dallimore, *George Whitefield* (Carlisle, Penn.: Banner of Truth, 1975), 1:196.

11

Truth & Love

There are two equally extreme misconceptions many people have concerning what it means to be a Christian or to live the Christian life. One view says, "It doesn't matter what you believe as long as you are sincere and loving." The other one says, "It doesn't matter how you live as long as you believe the truth." The reason why both views are just as wrong is because the Word of God binds both truth and love inseparably together. They are friends, not enemies.

GROUP DISCUSSION. Have you ever been in a situation where you felt torn between doing the right thing and the loving thing? Explain.

PERSONAL REFLECTION. Would you identify yourself as someone whose truth needs to be balanced by love or whose love needs to be balanced by truth?

Nestled between his introduction (vv. 1-3) and conclusion (vv. 12-13), John delivers a two-pronged message. The first demonstrates how this unity of truth and love applies first to our relationships within the church (vv. 4-6), and then to those outside of it (vv. 7-11). *Read 2 John.*

1. In the brief introductory address and greeting (vv. 1-3), notice how many times *truth* and *love* are mentioned together. What does it mean to love someone "in the truth" (v. 1)?

2. We tend to love only those Christians who agree with us or who we feel are compatible with us. But what does it mean to love them "because of the truth" (v. 2)?

3. How might our Christian fellowships be different if we took this teaching to heart?

4. In verses 4-6 the unity of truth and love is applied to our relationships within the church. What distinction is made between the commandment and the commandments?

5. How does our obedience to the commandments enable us to fulfill the commandment—and vice versa?

6. In verses 7-11 the unity of truth and love is applied to our relationships outside the church. By denying that Christ had come in the flesh (v. 7), what fundamental truths were the false teachers rejecting?

What are some modern counterparts to this kind of heresy?

_____

7. Obtaining a future reward for faithful service was a strong motivation for John (v. 8). In what sense does the prospect of receiving a reward from Jesus Christ motivate you to walk in truth and love?

_____

8. In view of the fact that these false teachers were traveling about from place to place, what specifically is being prohibited in verses 9-10?

_____

9. How does the reasoning of verse 11 help you to follow through on this instruction?

_____

10. What can you do to gain a better balance of love and truth in your relationships?

_____

Pray that your life would reveal a balance of love and truth.

Now or Later

After studying 2 John and reflecting on it, you might want to set down some standards for yourself regarding love and truth. Start by defining each. What does it mean to live and act in truth? What does it mean to live and act in love?

12

Opening Our
Hearts & Homes

3 John

Imagine living in a world where there were no bed and breakfasts, no hotels and headwaiters. If traveling evangelists and teachers were to come to your town, you would have the privilege of inviting them into your home for the night and giving them provisions for their journey. Such was the world of John and his readers. Their hospitality was one of the clearest testimonies of their love for the brethren and obedience to God. The same is true for us today.

GROUP DISCUSSION. When is showing hospitality difficult?

PERSONAL REFLECTION. How have you benefited from someone extending hospitality to you?

Following his introduction (v. 1), John's teaching on hospitality centers around his messages to or about the three personalities that he mentions: (1) Gaius, whom he counsels and exhorts (vv. 1-8, 11); (2) Diotrephes, whom he condemns (vv. 9-10); and (3) Demetrius, whom he commends (v. 12). *Read 3 John.*

1. Note the emphasis again on loving someone "in the truth" (v. 1; see also 2 John 1-2). Why must our love for fellow Christians be bound by the bond of truth?

How have you seen this to be true in your own experience?

_____

2. Why is Gaius an especially good example for us to follow in the Christian life (vv. 2-4)?

_____

3. What does it mean for us to be "walking in the truth" (vv. 3-4)?

_____

4. How are both love and faithfulness demonstrated in Christian hospitality (vv. 5-6)?

_____

5. What does it mean for us to show hospitality "in a manner worthy of God" (v. 6)?

_____

6. Why do you think Christian workers are to look to Christians for support and not to non-Christians (vv. 7-8)?

7. How are the actions of Diotrephes consistent with his true heart's desire (vv. 9-10)?

_____

8. If we desire to be first, how will that conflict with our ability to be loving?

_____

9. In contrast to Diotrephes, Demetrius was "well spoken of by everyone"(v. 12). If those who know you best were asked about your love and hospitality, what might they say?

_____

10. In light of this passage, what practical steps could you take to develop more of a ministry of hospitality?

_____

Pray for an open heart that will lead you to an open home.

Now or Later

On your own or in a separate session with your group, you might like to review 1, 2 and 3 John. Here are some questions to help you.

1. In 1 John there are no less than six references to the new birth (2:29; 3:9; 4:7; 5:1, 4, 18). According to John, what are some of the inevitable results of that experience?

_____

2. How would you respond to people who say that they are Christians regardless of how they live because they have professed faith in Christ?

3. Why is it impossible to have fellowship with those who have not truly been born of God's Spirit?

4. The enticements of the world seem to be getting stronger everyday. How do John's letters help us to realize and resist the world's influence?

5. How can John's letters help you to respond to the Mormons or Jehovah's Witnesses next time they knock on your door?

6. Concerning the Christian faith, F. F. Bruce has written, "Continuance is the test of reality."[1] How do John's letters support that statement, especially in view of his emphasis on "remaining" (or abiding) in Christ?

7. Professing Christians who choose to continue in sin are often described as "backsliders" or "carnal Christians" in an attempt to explain their behavior. What perspectives have John's letters given you about such people?

8. How have these letters changed your understanding of the Christian life?

9. How have they changed your understanding of living the Christian life?

---

[1]Bruce, *Epistles of John*, p. 69.

Leader's Notes

MY GRACE IS SUFFICIENT FOR YOU. (2 COR 12:9)

Leading a Bible discussion can be an enjoyable and rewarding experience. But it can also be *scary*—especially if you've never done it before. If this is your feeling, you're in good company. When God asked Moses to lead the Israelites out of Egypt, he replied, "O Lord, please send someone else to do it"! (Ex 4:13). It was the same with Solomon, Jeremiah and Timothy, but God helped these people in spite of their weaknesses, and he will help you as well.

You don't need to be an expert on the Bible or a trained teacher to lead a Bible discussion. The idea behind these inductive studies is that the leader guides group members to discover for themselves what the Bible has to say. This method of learning will allow group members to remember much more of what is said than a lecture would.

These studies are designed to be led easily. As a matter of fact, the flow of questions through the passage from observation to interpretation to application is so natural that you may feel that the studies lead themselves. This study guide is also flexible. You can use it with a variety of groups—student, professional, neighborhood or church groups. Each study takes forty-five to sixty minutes in a group setting.

There are some important facts to know about group dynamics and encouraging discussion. The suggestions listed below should enable you to effectively and enjoyably fulfill your role as leader.

Preparing for the Study

1. Ask God to help you understand and apply the passage in your own life. Unless this happens, you will not be prepared to lead others. Pray too for the various members of the group. Ask God to open your hearts to the message of his Word and motivate you to action.

2. Read the introduction to the entire guide to get an overview of the entire book and the issues which will be explored.

3. As you begin each study, read and reread the assigned Bible passage to familiarize yourself with it.

4. This study guide is based on the New International Version of the Bible. It will help you and the group if you use this translation as the basis for your study and discussion.

5. Carefully work through each question in the study. Spend time in meditation and reflection as you consider how to respond.

6. Write your thoughts and responses in the space provided in the study guide. This will help you to express your understanding of the passage clearly.

7. It might help to have a Bible dictionary handy. Use it to look up any unfamiliar words, names or places. (For additional help on how to study a passage, see chapter five of *How to Lead a LifeGuide Bible Study,* InterVarsity Press.)

8. Consider how you can apply the Scripture to your life. Remember that the group will follow your lead in responding to the studies. They will not go any deeper than you do.

9. Once you have finished your own study of the passage, familiarize yourself with the leader's notes for the study you are leading. These are designed to help you in several ways. First, they tell you the purpose the study guide author had in mind when writing the study. Take time to think through how the study questions work together to accomplish that purpose. Second, the notes provide you with additional background information or suggestions on group dynamics for various questions. This information can be useful when people have difficulty understanding or answering a question. Third, the leader's notes can alert you to potential problems you may encounter during the study.

10. If you wish to remind yourself of anything mentioned in the leader's notes, make a note to yourself below that question in the study.

Leading the Study

1. Begin the study on time. Open with prayer, asking God to help the group to understand and apply the passage.

2. Be sure that everyone in your group has a study guide. Encourage the group to prepare beforehand for each discussion by reading the introduction to the guide and by working through the questions in the study.

3. At the beginning of your first time together, explain that these studies are meant to be discussions, not lectures. Encourage the members of the group to participate. However, do not put pressure on those who may be hesitant to speak during the first few sessions. You may want to suggest the following guidelines to your group.

☐ Stick to the topic being discussed.

☐ Your responses should be based on the verses which are the focus of the discussion and not on outside authorities such as commentaries or speakers.

☐ These studies focus on a particular passage of Scripture. Only rarely should you refer to other portions of the Bible. This allows for everyone to participate in in-depth study on equal ground.

☐ Anything said in the group is considered confidential and will not be discussed outside the group unless specific permission is given to do so.

☐ We will listen attentively to each other and provide time for each person present to talk.

☐ We will pray for each other.

4. Have a group member read the introduction at the beginning of the discussion.

5. Every session begins with a group discussion question. The question or activity is meant to be used before the passage is read. The question introduces the theme of the study and encourages group members to begin to open up. Encourage as many members as possible to participate, and be ready to get the discussion going with your own response.

This section is designed to reveal where our thoughts or feelings need to be transformed by Scripture. That is why it is especially important not to read the passage before the discussion question is asked. The passage will tend to color the honest reactions people would otherwise give because they are, of course, supposed to think the way the Bible does.

You may want to supplement the group discussion question with an icebreaker to help people to get comfortable. See the community section of *Small Group Idea Book* for more ideas.

You also might want to use the personal reflection question with your group. Either allow a time of silence for people to respond individually or discuss it together.

6. Have a group member (or members if the passage is long) read aloud the passage to be studied. Then give people several minutes to read the passage again silently so that they can take it all in.

7. Question 1 will generally be an overview question designed to briefly survey the passage. Encourage the group to look at the whole passage, but try to avoid getting sidetracked by questions or issues that will be addressed later in the study.

8. As you ask the questions, keep in mind that they are designed to be used just as they are written. You may simply read them aloud. Or you may prefer to express them in your own words.

There may be times when it is appropriate to deviate from the study guide.

For example, a question may have already been answered. If so, move on to the next question. Or someone may raise an important question not covered in the guide. Take time to discuss it, but try to keep the group from going off on tangents.

9. Avoid answering your own questions. If necessary, repeat or rephrase them until they are clearly understood. Or point out something you read in the leader's notes to clarify the context or meaning. An eager group quickly becomes passive and silent if they think the leader will do most of the talking.

10. Don't be afraid of silence. People may need time to think about the question before formulating their answers.

11. Don't be content with just one answer. Ask, "What do the rest of you think?" or "Anything else?" until several people have given answers to the question.

12. Acknowledge all contributions. Try to be affirming whenever possible. Never reject an answer. If it is clearly off-base, ask, "Which verse led you to that conclusion?" or again, "What do the rest of you think?"

13. Don't expect every answer to be addressed to you, even though this will probably happen at first. As group members become more at ease, they will begin to truly interact with each other. This is one sign of healthy discussion.

14. Don't be afraid of controversy. It can be very stimulating. If you don't resolve an issue completely, don't be frustrated. Move on and keep it in mind for later. A subsequent study may solve the problem.

15. Periodically summarize what the group has said about the passage. This helps to draw together the various ideas mentioned and gives continuity to the study. But don't preach.

16. At the end of the Bible discussion you may want to allow group members a time of quiet to work on an idea under "Now or Later." Then discuss what you experienced. Or you may want to encourage group members to work on these ideas between meetings. Give an opportunity during the session for people to talk about what they are learning.

17. Conclude your time together with conversational prayer, adapting the prayer suggestion at the end of the study to your group. Ask for God's help in following through on the commitments you've made.

18. End on time.

Many more suggestions and helps are found in *How to Lead a LifeGuide Bible Study.*

Components of Small Groups

A healthy small group should do more than study the Bible. There are four components to consider as you structure your time together.

Nurture. Small groups help us to grow in our knowledge and love of God. Bible study is the key to making this happen and is the foundation of your small group.

Community. Small groups are a great place to develop deep friendships with other Christians. Allow time for informal interaction before and after each study. Plan activities and games that will help you get to know each other. Spend time having fun together—going on a picnic or cooking dinner together.

Worship and prayer. Your study will be enhanced by spending time praising God together in prayer or song. Pray for each other's needs—and keep track of how God is answering prayer in your group. Ask God to help you to apply what you are learning in your study.

Outreach. Reaching out to others can be a practical way of applying what you are learning, and it will keep your group from becoming self-focused. Host a series of evangelistic discussions for your friends or neighbors. Clean up the yard of an elderly friend. Serve at a soup kitchen together, or spend a day working on a Habitat house.

Many more suggestions and helps in each of these areas are found in *Small Group Idea Book*. Information on building a small group can be found in *Small Group Leaders' Handbook* and *The Big Book on Small Groups* (both from Inter-Varsity Press). Reading through one of these books would be worth your time.

Study 1. 1 John 1. Fellowship & Forgiveness.

Purpose: To understand the basis for having true fellowship with other Christians and with God.

Question 3. John's initial emphasis on the incarnation of Christ is due to the fact that his readers were being confronted with an early form of heresy known as Gnosticism (see the introduction to the guide). Its central teaching was that the spirit is entirely good and matter is entirely evil, a type of dualism resulting in a denial of Christ's true humanity. This particular false teaching provides the backdrop for much of John's letter (see 2:22-23; 4:2-3; 5:6-8).

Question 4. It is important to note that in the New Testament the term *fellowship* is used to refer to a participation, or partnership, with those who share something in common. In verse 3 fellowship is based on a common faith in Christ as the incarnate Son of God. Therefore, there can be no spiritual fellowship with any individual or group that does not share this common faith in Jesus Christ as the God-man.

Question 5. If fellowship can only be experienced by those who possess something in common, then those who are in fellowship with God will manifest a likeness to his character (vv. 5-7) and a readiness to confess sin (vv. 8-10). Without such evidence there is *no* fellowship with God, regardless of one's claims (vv. 6, 8, 10). This is the first occurrence of the ethical, or moral, test within 1 John. Like the prologue, this passage is also designed to refute the false teaching of Gnosticism, which denied that obedience to God's commands had any bearing on one's relationship to God. (See "Background to 1 John" in the introduction.)

Question 7. If you need to restate the question, you might say, "Is John describing Christians who are either in or out of fellowship with God, or Christians and those who really do not know God at all? Explain." It is important to remember that two lifestyles are being contrasted in these verses: one is characterized by error and sin, the other by truth and righteousness. In view of the other similar contrasts that will emerge in this letter (2:3-6; 3:6-9) and the terms that are used in this passage to describe those who do not enjoy fellowship with God (vv. 6, 8, 10), it seems clear that John's contrast is between true Christians and those who merely profess to be Christians.

Question 8. Verse 9 is often used to teach that our moment-by-moment fellowship with God is dependent on us confessing our sins. According to this view, Christians who deny their sins are out of fellowship with God, while those who confess their sins remain in fellowship with him.

But in view of the apparent contrast between Christians and non-Christians within the preceding verses (vv. 6-7), it is more likely that John has the same contrast in mind in verses 8-10. Just as our moral lifestyle determines the reality of our claim to have fellowship with God, so also does our attitude toward sin. If we confess the guilt of our sin, John assures us that we have entered into a saving fellowship with God (v. 9). But if we deny that we are guilty of sin, John concludes that we have no saving fellowship with God at all (vv. 8, 10).

Study 2. 1 John 2:1-11. Talking & Walking the Truth.

Purpose: To realize that we must look beyond what we say to what we do in order to be certain about the reality of our faith.

Question 1. The word translated "atoning sacrifice" (v. 2) best expresses the idea of propitiation. This simply means that when Christ died as a sacrifice for sin, he "satisfied" God's justice, which demanded that his wrath be poured out against those who through sin have violated his law (cf. 3:4). As a result, God's wrath is now turned away from the sinner so that he is free to forgive sins. It is precisely because of this work of atonement that Christ can and does perform his work of advocacy on our behalf.

Question 3. Be sure to keep in mind that what is being described within these verses is our general lifestyle, not an occasional breaking of God's commands. Certainly Christians can and do sin, as John indicates in verses 1-2.

Question 4. Not only does obedience to Christ's commands demonstrate that we know him, it gives clear evidence that we now love God and are in union with Christ. Grammatically speaking, it is possible for "God's love" (v. 5) to have one of two meanings: (a) God's love for us, which is made complete when it moves us to obedience; (b) our love for God, which is made complete when it is demonstrated by obedience.

Question 6. Although the biblical command to love is old, Jesus Christ has invested it with a richer and deeper meaning. The old command was "Love your neighbor as yourself" (Lev 19:18). The new command is "Love one another. As I have loved you, so you must love one another" (Jn 13:34). This command is new for two reasons. First, it is new in its object: "love one another"—that is, other Christians. Second, it is new in its standard: "as I have loved you." Christ's death on the cross becomes the new measure of our love. As John says later in his letter, "This is how we know what love is: Jesus Christ laid down his life for us. And we ought to lay down our lives for our brothers"(1 Jn 3:16).

Question 8. It is clear from these verses that our love for fellow believers is the evidence that we have eternal life. Hatred for members of the Christian community indicates that one "remains in death" (3:14) and does not have eternal life (3:15); he is "still in the darkness" (2:9). Love, on the other hand, is the evidence that we are "born of God" (3:10) and have "passed from death to life" (3:14); we are "in the light" (2:9). This is the first occurrence of what has been called the social test within 1 John. Like the moral test, its purpose is to validate the reality of our profession of faith in Christ.

Study 3. 1 John 2:12-17. Encouragement & Warning.

Purpose: To encourage us in view of our spiritual attainments and to warn us in view of our spiritual enemies.

Question 1. It may be helpful to review with the group the somewhat severe statements that John has just made concerning obedience (2:3-6) and love (2:7-11): "He does not mean to give his readers the impression that he thinks they are in darkness or that he doubts the reality of their faith. It is the false teachers whom he regards as spurious, not the loyal members of the church. So he digresses to tell them his view of their Christian standing" (Stott, *Epistles of John*, p. 95).

Question 2. There have been various suggestions concerning how to interpret these figurative expressions. Probably the best approach is to understand the reference to the "little children" as one which embraces all the readers (see 2:1); the "fathers" as representing those who are older in the faith; the "young men" as those who are younger in the faith.

Question 3. These young Christians overcame the evil one because they were strong, and they were strong because the truth of God's Word was continually living within them. Likewise, the only hope we have for overcoming the deceptive tactics and schemes of Satan is in knowing and abiding in the truths of God's Word.

Question 4. Remember that the term *world* has numerous meanings in the New Testament, depending on the context in which it is found. Here John is emphasizing the way in which the world system thinks and acts apart from God, as this context clearly indicates.

Question 5. There is a fundamental antagonism between God and the world system. Because love for the world and love for God are mutually exclusive (v. 15), and because the sinful attitudes in the world are not from God (v. 16), the world and all that is in it is in opposition to God. To love the world, therefore, is to love the enemy of God.

Question 7. Worldliness has to do with our sinful attitudes toward material possessions rather than the material possessions themselves. It is the craving for and boasting in the things of this world that John specifically has in view.

Study 4. 1 John 2:18-27. How Important Is Theology?

Purpose: To confirm that the teaching ministry of the Holy Spirit is our defense against those who would have us believe that Jesus is not the Christ.

Question 1. The meaning of the word *antichrist* is important to understand. It is formed by joining two words: *Christ* and the prefix *anti*, which in this context means "against." As "antichrists," their false teaching concentrates on opposing and denying the truth that the man Jesus is the divine, eternal Christ (v. 22). They are identified "not as those who are outside the Church, but as those who at least for a time were within it. In other words, they are not the outright pagan opponents of Christianity but rather those who were attempting to destroy the faith from within by pretending to be Christians" (James M. Boice, *The Epistles of John* [Grand Rapids, Mich.: Zondervan, 1983], pp. 85-86).

Question 4. While some will certainly disagree, the teaching of verse 19 "is built upon the principle that genuine believers persevere in the faith and in their association with other believers" (Donald Burdick, *The Letters of John the Apostle* [Chicago: Moody Press, 1985], p. 195). Since those who are born of God are characterized by overcoming faith (1 Jn 5:4), they cannot apostatize, or depart from the faith. While apostasy is possible for those who have merely professed saving faith in Christ, it is not possible for genuine believers. Saving faith enables us to continue in our faith and in our identity with others of like faith. Therefore, if one defects from the fellowship, it is a clear indication that he or she was never in the faith.

Question 5. The indwelling presence of the Holy Spirit is the fundamental means of understanding the truth of God's Word and of using what we learn to combat heresy. Specifically, John is referring to the Spirit's ministry of illumination, or the revealing of God's truth to our hearts (see 1 Cor 2:12, 15-16).

Question 6. This is the first occurrence of the doctrinal—or christological—test within the epistle. The purpose is not only to provide assurance to the readers that they are in the faith but to expose the false teachers for who they really are—unbelieving heretics.

Question 7. The second way that we combat doctrinal error is by holding fast to the apostolic truths of the gospel which we have heard from the beginning of our Christian experience, as opposed to neglecting them in search of some new teaching. As Paul told Timothy: "But as for you, continue in what you have learned and have become convinced of" (2 Tim 3:14). It is this continuance in the truths of God's Word that assures us of God's promise to us: eternal life.

Question 9. In light of the context, both here and throughout the letter, abiding in Christ is continuing, or remaining, in the truths about Christ. It is, therefore, the mark of *all* genuine believers, not just a select few. Remaining in Christ means persevering in the faith.

Study 5. 1 John 2:28—3:10. Like Father, Like Son.

Purpose: To demonstrate that those who are born of a righteous God will live a righteous life.

Question 1. In these verses we now have the second cycle of tests beginning to unfold. Here the test is the same one that was first introduced in 1:5-10 and then in 2:3-6. It is the moral test, or the test of obedience to Christ's commands. The emphasis, however, is slightly different in that John now introduces the concept of being born of God as the reason for the practice of righteousness. It is this birth from above which imparts the life of God within us that is inevitably responsible for our family likeness (2:29; 3:9; see also 4:7-8; 5:1, 4, 18).

Question 6. The point of this question is to underscore how so many today underestimate the seriousness of sin. It is not merely "missing the mark" of God's righteousness, or departing from what is right; it is an active rebellion against God's revealed will and a deliberate violation of his holy law.

Acknowledging this is absolutely fundamental to living a holy life: "He that wishes to attain right views about Christian holiness must begin by examining the vast and solemn subject of sin" (J. C. Ryle, *Holiness* [Grand Rapids, Mich.: Baker, 1979], p. 1).

Question 7. It's impossible because of who Christ is and the purpose of his "appearing." In his nature there is no indwelling sin (v. 5); he is righteous (v. 7). His purpose in coming was to remove sins (v. 5) or to destroy the work of the devil, who is the source of all sin (v. 8). Therefore, it is impossible for those who have come to know Christ to continue in sin.

Question 8. The moral deception that is in view here is just as dangerous as the doctrinal deception that was addressed in the previous passage (see 2:26). It comes under the broad banner of "antinomianism," which says that because we are under the grace of God, we no longer are bound to any moral law. In other words, these false teachers were emphasizing that it is possible to *be* righteous without ever attempting to *practice* righteousness.

Question 10. One of the best explanations of this difficult verse comes from John Stott: "The new birth involves the acquisition of a new nature through the implanting within us of the very seed or life-giving power of God. Birth from God is a deep, radical, inward transformation. Moreover, the new nature received at the new birth remains. It exerts a strong internal pressure towards holiness. It is the abiding influence of His seed within everyone who is born of God, which enables John to affirm without fear of contradiction that he cannot go on living in sin" (Stott, *Epistles of John,* p. 127).

Study 6. 1 John 3:11-24. Blessed Assurance.

Purpose: To show that the evidence of a right standing before God is a sacrificial love for other Christians.

Question 2. As in 1 John 2:7-11, John is contrasting love with hatred. But here he uses Cain as the example of hatred toward his brother (Abel), who is a prototype of the world's hatred towards Christians (v. 13). This contrast cannot be minimized. It has the effect of saying, "Whatever may be the attitudes and actions of the world, we who are Christians are different; we love one another. *This* is evidence of the fact that we are God's children" (Boice, *Epistles of John,* p. 115).

Question 3. Assurance of salvation comes through a threefold witness: (a) the testimony of God's Word (1 Jn 5:10-12); (b) the testimony of the Holy Spirit (1 Jn 3:24); and (c) the testimony of a changed life, which is John's overwhelming emphasis in this letter. First John 3:14-15 is but one application of this latter testimony.

Question 4. If love is a test of genuine salvation, then it is crucial to discuss John's test of genuine love within these verses. The meaning of love in modern culture has become so debased and diluted that just about anyone can claim to have love and therefore be a Christian.

Question 6. It is important to realize that the beginning phrase of verse 19, "this then is how we know," points back to what has just been stated in verses 16-18. The next verse (20) then goes on to give us an additional reason for our assurance.

Question 10. "But if we intend to obey His commandments, let us see what He commands. He does not separate faith from love, but demands of us that both . . . mutually embrace one another. This is why he puts the word *commandment* in the singular. But this is a remarkable passage, for he defines clearly and briefly what the complete perfection of a holy life consists in" (John Calvin, *The First Epistle of John* [Grand Rapids, Mich.: Baker, 1979], p. 281).

Study 7. 1 John 4:1-12. Discernment & Devotion.

Purpose: To demonstrate that the indwelling presence of God's Spirit enables us to confess Jesus as Christ and to love one another.

Question 1. In giving us a further explanation of the doctrinal test, John begins by again reminding us that not every "spirit" is to be believed. The word *spirit* means either an utterance or a person "inspired by a spirit," and points us to the fact that a person's teaching is inspired either by God or by Satan. The danger of demonic deception cannot be underestimated within the church today.

Question 3. Opinions will vary as to who the modern-day representatives of "the spirit of the antichrist" would be. Some may cite members of major cults, such as Mormons, Jehovah's Witnesses and Christian Scientists. Others may also cite those who embrace various forms of liberal Protestant theology and who are now denying the deity of Christ from the pulpits of mainline denominations.

Question 5. In verses 1-3 the emphasis has been on the false teachers—what are they saying? But in these verses the emphasis is on the hearers—who is listening to what they are saying? Both the "content of the their teaching" and the "character of their audience" are decisive tests for determining if they are from God (Stott, *Epistles of John*, p. 152).

Question 6. This passage marks the beginning of the third cycle of tests that John has been using throughout this epistle (see "Background to 1 John" in the introduction). It is also the third major discussion of love as the social test of genuine faith (see 1 Jn 2:7-11; 3:11-18).

Question 9. According to 3:16-18, genuine love will express itself in practical deeds of love. This is the "completed" love of verse 12. John's point is simply this: whenever we actively demonstrate love to other believers, God is seen in our lives because he is the source of our love. In this sense, then, the God whom "no one has ever seen" is seen in our midst. His love is completed because its goal is realized, enabling us to love others.

Study 8. 1 John 4:13-21. Fear's Remedy.

Purpose: To demonstrate that God's love for us enables us to stand confidently before him without fear.

Question 1. These three grounds for assurance could be termed the *internal* witness (the presence of the Holy Spirit, v. 13); the *external* witness (the confession that Jesus is the Christ, vv. 14-15); the *evidential* witness (the fruits of the Christian life, in this case love for one another, v. 16). All three are essential for Christian assurance.

Question 3. It is simply not enough to affirm the truth that Jesus is God. Our creed must be backed by our conduct, which in turn is the result of knowing and experiencing God's love.

Question 5. If we are Christlike in our love for one another, this is confirming evidence that God, who is love, lives in us. For that reason genuine love is grounds for assurance on the day of judgment.

Question 7. One of the best ways to gain a deeper appreciation of God's love for us is to meditate on what John has already told us: God's love is the reason for our redemption (1 Jn 4:8-10) and our adoption into his family (1 Jn 3:1). In light of such love for us, how is it possible for us not to love others?

Question 8. The commandment to which John refers in verse 21 is the one that originally came from God (Deut 6:4-5; Lev 19:18) and was then used by Christ to teach that love was the foundation of Old Testament law (Mt 22:37-40).

Study 9. 1 John 5:1-12. Faith Is the Victory.

Purpose: To demonstrate that faith in the incarnate Son of God is the means of overcoming the errors and falsehoods of the world system.

Question 3. The point of verses 3-4 is not that the commandments themselves are easy to obey; rather they become easy to obey because of the enabling presence of the indwelling Spirit, brought about through the new birth. The reason for the struggle, then, is due to the ongoing, internal conflict between flesh and spirit.

Question 4. Doctrinally, we triumph over the world's opposition to God's truth (4:1-6) by believing in Jesus as the incarnate Son of God. Morally, too, we triumph over the world's selfish, unloving lifestyle (2:15-17) by faith in Christ, the fruit of which is love for the brethren. This twofold victory over the world is initiated by the new birth and is the progressive experience of everyone born of God.

Question 5. With this emphasis, these false teachers maintained that Jesus was born and died only as a man. Hence, they denied both the incarnation and crucifixion of Jesus as the God-man. Such a denial strikes at the very heart of the gospel message, since only the God-man can atone for our sin and at the same time satisfy God's wrath against sin (2:2; 4:10).

Question 6. The baptism of Jesus testifies to the reality of the incarnation because at that time the Holy Spirit declared, "This is my Son, whom I love; with him I am well pleased" (Mt 3:17). John's primary point is that this same Son of God who was baptized in the Jordan was also the One who died on the cross. This is the One whom believers acknowledge to be the Son of God (v. 5).

Question 7. In addition to the water and blood, the Holy Spirit also testifies that Jesus is the Son of God. The Spirit did this when he descended on Jesus at his baptism (see Jn 1:32-34) and continues to do this through the ministry of God's Word (see Jn 15:26).

Question 9. In contrast to the previous three witnesses, this fourth witness is experienced only by believers. "When a person places his faith in the incarnate Christ, he experiences eternal life with all that such an experience involves (God's Spirit bearing witness with his spirit)" (Burdick, *Epistles of John*, p. 381).

Study 10. 1 John 5:13-21. What We Know as Christians.

Purpose: To teach us that God has not only given us assurances of knowing him but of receiving answers from him in prayer.

Question 1. It would be helpful at this point to highlight the three tests that John has been weaving throughout this letter. For example, assurance can be tested by obedience to Christ's commandments (2:3-6), love for the brethren (3:11-15) and belief that Jesus is the incarnate Son of God (4:1-6).

Question 3. These two passages represent two of the major conditions for answered prayer in the New Testament and, therefore, ought to be emphasized. Compare also John 15:7.

Questions 4-6. Verses 16-17 are two of the most difficult verses in all of the New Testament. The interpretive issues are complex, but basically there are two broad viewpoints concerning the meaning of "a sin that leads to death." The first view is that believers who continue to live in sin experience the divine discipline of physical death. If we were to pray for their spiritual restoration, then we should not be surprised if our prayers were not answered. Our request would not be according to God's will. Certainly other passages teach that such divine discipline does occur (see 1 Cor 11:30), but the difficulty here is that John has repeatedly emphasized that genuine believers cannot continue in sin (see 3:9). In fact, he says this very same thing in the next verse (18). Therefore, this is probably not the best interpretation.

The second view is that nonbelievers who are characterized by the adamant denial of the truth and willful immorality that John has been exposing throughout this letter will certainly experience spiritual death. If we were to pray for their salvation, then we should not be surprised that our request was not answered because it would not be according to God's will. Such a persistent denial of Christ by those who were once professing members of the church (see 2:19) is nothing short of apostasy and, therefore, places them beyond the saving grace of God (see Heb 6:4-6). This seems to be the best understanding in light of the context of the letter. To the objection that the sin unto death cannot be committed by a non-Christian because of the use of the word *brother,* John Stott offers a helpful explanation: "If the sin is . . . committed by a hardened unbeliever, how can John call him a 'brother'? To be exact, he does not. It is the one whose sin is 'not unto death' who is termed a brother; he whose sin is 'unto death' is neither named nor described" (*Epistles of John,* p. 189).

With either view the point of the passage is the same: there are certain requests that will not be answered the way we would like simply because they are not in accordance with God's will. Therefore, the assurance of verses 14-15 is qualified.

Question 8. There are three great words of certainty that are emphasized in this letter: we *are* children of God (3:1); he who has the Son *has* eternal life (5:12); we *know* him who is true (5:19). How fitting, then, for this letter to end in verses 18-20 on such a repeated emphasis of assurance.

Study 11. 2 John. Truth & Love.

Purpose: To demonstrate how our love for others is to be guided and governed by the truth.

Question 1. As the remainder of this letter will reveal, these readers had been exercising love at the expense of truth. In particular, they had been indiscriminately practicing hospitality to all traveling teachers, including those who were rejecting fundamental doctrines of the faith. To love "in the truth," therefore, is to demonstrate a love that is consistent with the truth; it is a love that is governed and guided by the truth.

Question 3. One of the sad commentaries in so many circles of fellowship is that culture, ethnicity, race and language have created walls of separation that we as Christians are content to accept. But to love one another for no other reason than "because of the truth" means that we must be willing to transcend these natural barriers so that we can become bound to all types of Christians by the special bond of truth that we share in Christ.

Question 4. The "commandments" are all of the specific requirements that explain how we are to go about fulfilling the "command" to love one another. A helpful explanation of these verses can be found in Romans 13:8-10.

Question 6. These are the same false teachers who formed the background to much of what John wrote in his first letter (see 1 Jn 2:18-19; 4:2-3) They are "antichrists" in the sense that they deny Christ's incarnation and thus his deity. Here they are further described as those who "run ahead" of the elementary truths of the gospel. Some of their modern-day counterparts are identified in the leader's notes for study seven, question 3.

Question 8. Hospitality is the issue that John is addressing. Such instruction, therefore, would not prohibit us from greeting or even conversing with those who come to us with this teaching. What it does prohibit is providing them with any support for their work, such as housing and food. Such a prohibition, then, is a practical application of love that is guided and governed by the truth.

Question 9. "False teaching which denies Christ and so robs men of the Father is not just an unfortunate error; it is a 'wicked work.' . . . It may send souls to eternal ruin. If, then, we do not wish to further such wicked work (to become 'an accomplice in his wicked deeds' NEB), we must give no encouragement to the worker" (Stott, *Epistle of John*, pp. 214-15).

Study 12. 3 John. Opening Our Hearts & Homes.

Purpose: To demonstrate how our commitment to the truth is to be manifested by our love for others.

Question 2. "Walking" in the truth is far different than merely talking about the truth. It is one thing to know the Christian jargon; it is another to live the Christian life. Gaius, therefore, is an excellent illustration of the importance of our "walk matching our talk." See especially 1 John 2:3-6; 4:20-21.

Question 4. Because hospitality is a frequently repeated commandment elsewhere (Rom 12:13; 1 Pet 4:9; Heb 13:2) as well as in this passage (v. 8), it is a very practical demonstration of our faithfulness to God's Word. It is also a tangible expression of our love for God's people (see 1 Jn 3:16-18).

Question 5. This is the kind of treatment toward others that pleases God and brings praise to his name (see Col 1:10; 1 Thess 2:12). In practical terms, this means that our hospitality is to be done willingly, generously and, above all else, lovingly, not begrudgingly (see 1 Pet 4:9).

Question 7. What is most significant to note about Diotrephes is that he is not one of the false teachers John has been denouncing in these letters. There is no suggestion that he has disagreed with John on any basic point of doctrine. His root problem is personal ambition, which has led him to resist apostolic authority. Everything else in these verses is merely the result of this problem.

Question 9. Demetrius serves as an illustration of the exhortation in verse 11: "[Imitate] what is good." In contrast, Diotrephes is the embodiment of what John has in view in the first part of verse 11: "Do not imitate what is evil."

Now or Later

Question 1. A twofold emphasis is placed on the new birth in these passages: (1) Certain things are inevitably true of everyone who has been born of God (3:9; 5:4, 18); (2) everyone who has certain fruits in his or her life is identified as being born of God (2:29; 4:7; 5:1). Both perspectives demonstrate the necessary cause-effect relationship between the new birth and the fruits of that birth.

Question 3. The root meaning of the term *fellowship* is a "sharing" in that which is common. Our common faith, based on a common commitment to the truths of the gospel, makes our fellowship with one another possible. See especially 1 John 1:3-4 in light of 2:18-19.

Question 6. The most explicit teaching within these letters in support of such a statement is found in 1 John 2:19. Of the false teachers, John says, "If they had belonged to us, they would have *remained* with us" (my emphasis). This same emphasis on "remaining" or "abiding" in the truth appears over twenty other times within these letters (1 Jn 2:6, 10, 14, 17, 24, 27, 28; 3:6, 9, 14, 15, 17, 24; 4:12, 13, 15, 16; 2 Jn 2, 9).

Question 7. Certainly Christians can and do fall into sin. What John has been stating, however, is that they cannot continue in such sin. The assurance that we have been born of God's Spirit rests on our obedience to Christ's commands, love for the brethren and continued belief in the truth about God's Son. Saving faith, therefore, is a persevering faith—one that continues in holiness and faith.

Ronald A. Blankley is pastor of Bethel Evangelical Free Church in Fair Lawn, New Jersey, and is on the faculty at New York School of the Bible in New York City. He is a graduate of Dallas Theological Seminary.